D1548580

ANOTHER LANGUAGE OF FLOWERS

Another Language of Flowers

PAINTINGS

Dorothea Tanning

POEMS

JAMES MERRILL • HARRY MATHEWS • ROSANNA WARREN

DEBORA GREGER • ADRIENNE RICH • ANTHONY HECHT

RICHARD HOWARD • J. D. McCLATCHY • W. S. MERWIN

JOHN ASHBERY • STEPHEN YENSER

BRENDA SHAUGHNESSY

GEORGE BRAZILLER PUBLISHER   New York

The biographical material on the poets appears courtesy of
the Academy of American Poets.

First published in 1998 by George Braziller, Inc.

© 1998 by Dorothea Tanning
The copyright to each poem is held by its author.

All rights reserved. No part of this publication may be
reproduced in any form or by any means without prior
permission in writing from the publisher.

For information, please address the publisher:
George Braziller, Inc.
171 Madison Avenue
New York, NY 10016

Library of Congress Cataloging in Publication Data:
Tanning, Dorothea, 1910–
Another language of flowers / paintings, Dorothea Tanning ; poems, James Merrill . . . [et al.].
p.   cm.
ISBN 0-8076-1448-3 (hardback)
1. Tanning, Dorothea, 1910–   . 2. Flowers in art. 3. Flowers—Poetry.
I. Title.
ND237.T34A4 1998
759.13—dc21   98–41304
                CIP

Designed by Ink, Inc.
Printed and bound by LS Graphic, Inc. / Grafica Comense srl - Como (Italy)
First edition

CONTENTS

THE ARTIST

IN THE FALL of 1997 I visited DOROTHEA TANNING's studio several times during the painting of the canvases that are now reproduced in this book. Watching them emerge, I marveled at the creative energy she sustained over the course of the year and at her determination to complete the work she had envisioned. My admiration for the artist's drive, and the work's progression, canvas after canvas, gave me precious insight into their genesis and their realization.

Dorothea Tanning has been making art for more than fifty years. Or, if years have import, she has been an artist from early childhood. Whatever passed through her consciousness was coaxed into a mold and shaped by imagination. So that her painting, sculpting, writing, ballet designing for Balanchine; her Paris book collaborations in etching and lithography; her jewelry sculpture and even the architectural adventure of designing a house in the south of France, have all been undertaken with a natural creative spirit.

Born in a small town in Illinois, eighty-eight years ago, she has never stopped producing the works by which she is increasingly known, whether they are the early, Surrealist paintings of the nineteen forties and fifties, the more enigmatic, fragmented, later paintings, or the cloth sculpture of the seventies, where the lines and modeling challenge their materials and give them a poignant reality.

Often written about (a comprehensive monograph issued by the present publisher appeared in 1995), yet rarely seen, the work is complex and hard to classify. As John Russell said in that volume, "Seen through the prism of the entire oeuvre one recognizes a blueprint for a totally personal view of the world, a proposal, as remarkable for its daring as for its difference, to bring the other, interior world into view.... Her works belong to no place, to no school, almost to no time...."

One senses, in Dorothea Tanning's approach to painting, a respect, and even a tenderness, for the element she is at pains to portray. These twelve paintings, which she calls her foray into an imaginary botany, wonderfully fulfill their destiny. They are the testimony of a powerful vision.

G.B.

ANOTHER LANGUAGE OF FLOWERS

A NEW HYBRID OF FLOWER has always occasioned celebration by gardeners and amateur botanists everywhere. It is hard to think of anything more innocently irresistible than a flower, new or familiar, while an imagined one must surely bring a special frisson of excitement. Or so I thought, on the day in June when such a flower grew in my mind's eye and demanded to be painted. Once begun, the experiment widened into an entire garden. They bloomed all at once, as if to race with a short summer, and soon there were twelve canvases of twelve flowers waiting to be named. I had been thinking about the old custom of the language of flowers, so dear to poets—deprived as they were of telephones and faxes and e-mail—Keats and Wordsworth and Shelley and all the others, friends and lovers of their time and before. That each flower, sent or carried to its destination, had its own, and known, meaning was a source of pleasurable communication for them, needed and heeded. What better way to say "Beware!" or "Someone loves you," than with a poem hidden in the heart of a flower? Perhaps we need it now, *another* language of flowers, one for us, for now, an urgent pause, however brief.

So when these twelve painted blossoms revealed themselves on canvas it was immediately clear to me that each one needed a name and a meaning that only a poet could give; because this was to be that new, other language of flowers with all the import that the term implies. And so it happens that they have had the good fortune to be identified and blessed with the words of twelve poets, friends of the artist, who have given them their voices: *Another Language of Flowers*, for another garden.

As for the paintings, they were done between June 1997 and April 1998. They are naked, precise depictions of visions as real to me as botanical specimens are to the scientist. Prepared for with preliminary sketches—a number of which are reproduced in this book—as touchstones on the way to the flowers' inceptions, the sketches are this artist's way of coaxing image from idea. For some flowers one sketch was enough, and then, for others, there were four or five

before the flower emerged. Thus, each painting begins with its sketch and the

date on which it was begun, as one notes the day a bulb was planted.

Maps of a possible geography, a lexicon with just twelve entries, these

flowers are scrupulously delineated by a happy lexicographer, sensing them like

a wafture, an interruption, a bit of chamber music offered in a spirit of high-

hearted fidelity to conjuration. Their ambition, if ambition can apply, is not to

rival nature's marvels—an unthinkable thought—but to pay them homage, the

imagination itself being, after all, one of those marvels. In painting these flowers

my reward, then, was the simple delight that came with making them happen.

Among the flowers' poems are some lines by James Merrill. Even though

he is gone, I couldn't imagine doing anything like this without him.

Dorothea Tanning

June 8, 1997

Merrillium trovatum

A door just floats ajar.
The stillness trembles like a star.
A wish. Come true? Here's where to learn.

James Merrill

(from *Declaration Day)*

PLATE I

June 23

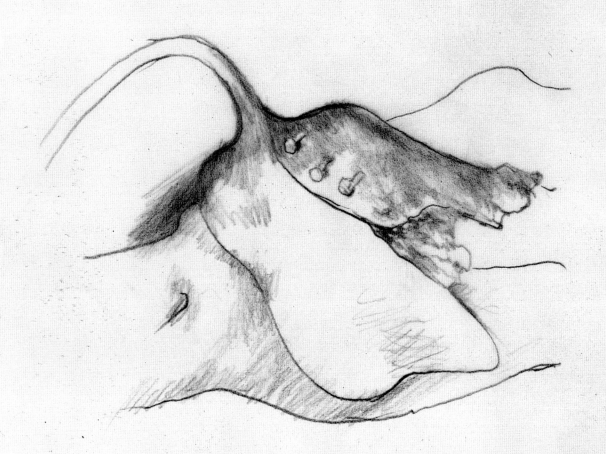

Agripedium vorax Saccherii

(Clog Herb)

A maudlin nectary for your must,
A yellow pillow for your rest,
A thick root for your rust.

Harry Mathews

PLATE 2

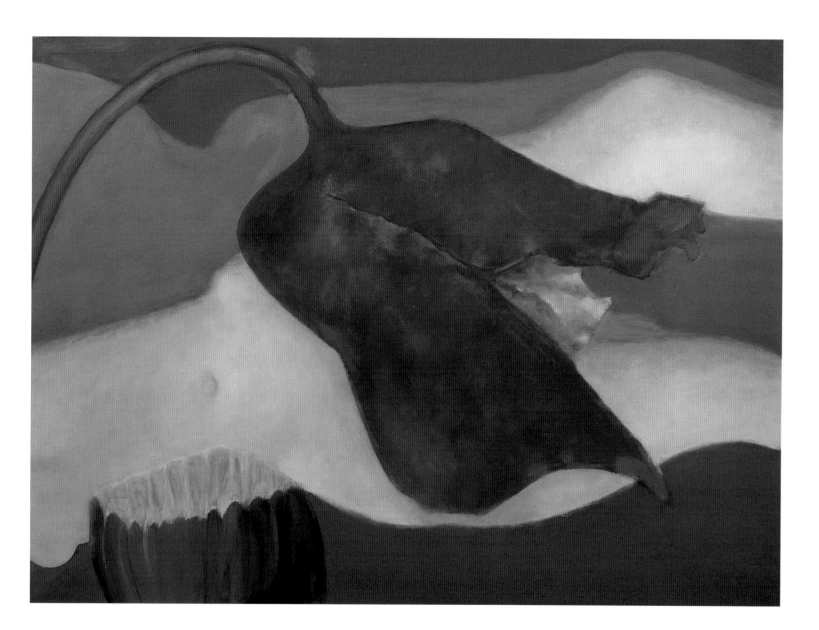

July 8

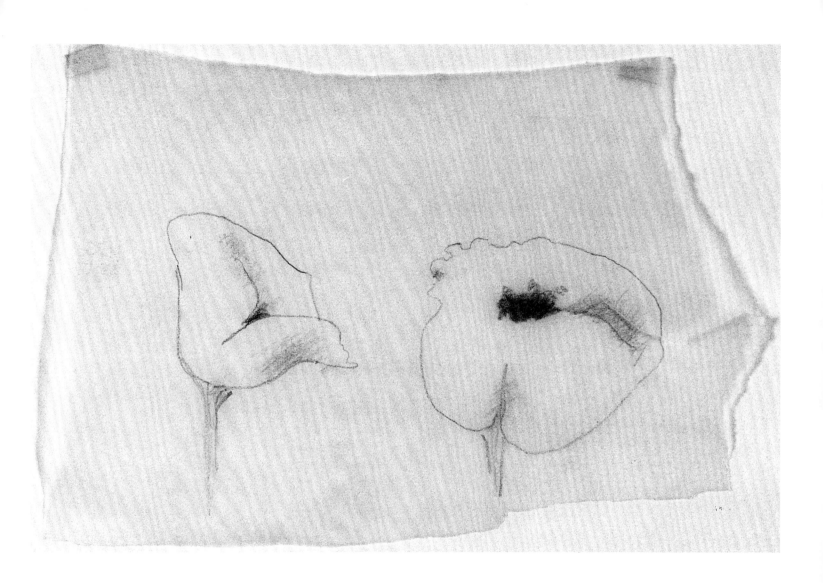

Siderium exaltatum

(Starry Venusweed)

Tapering to char
the wicks seek consummation
beyond the body:
one roused from ovaries of light,
one from a dying star.

Rosanna Warren

PLATE 3

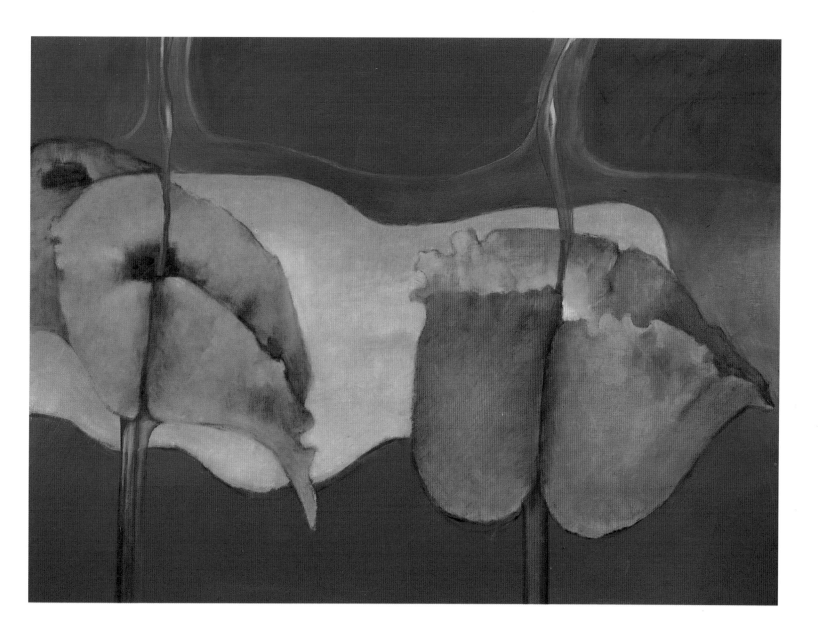

July 24

Zephirium apochripholiae

(Windwort)

I am an eclipse in full flower.
The dark shadow of the earth,
the black heart of the sun
lean against me.

Debora Greger

PLATE 4

August 9

SKETCH 5

Pictor mysteriosa

(Burnt Umbrage)

Pistil, stamen and bract
but never abstract:
the flower becomes the eye
we see her by.

Adrienne Rich

PLATE 5

August 30

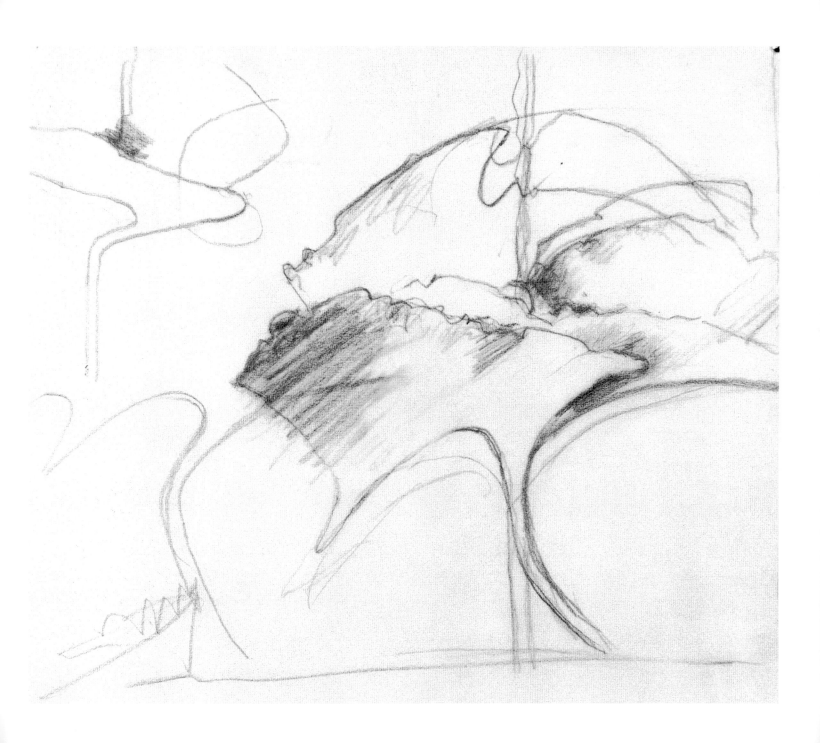

Asclepius formidabilis

(Griefbane)

To be preferred above base metal,
    I am a gold that glisters not:
    Exsufflicated mind and spirit
Of Greece and Keats's earthen pot.

Anthony Hecht

PLATE 6

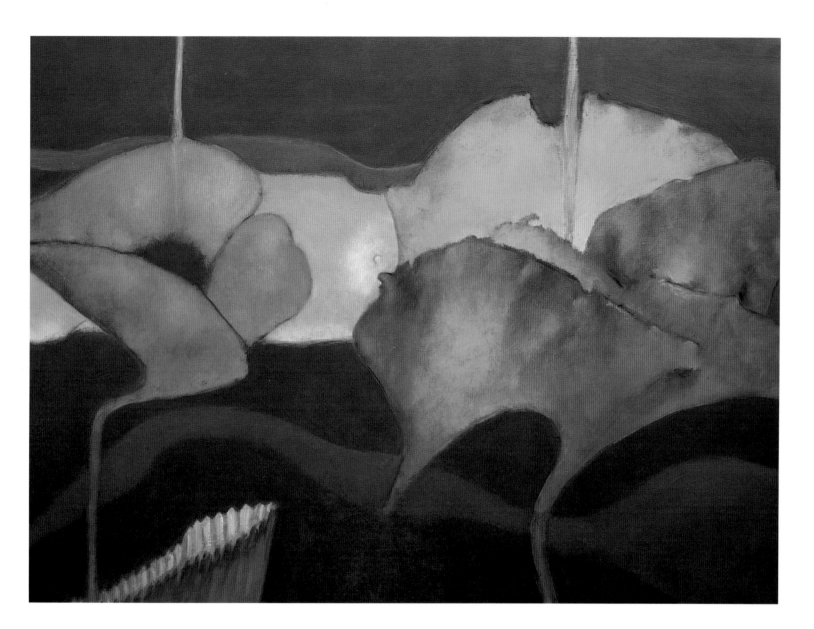

September 16

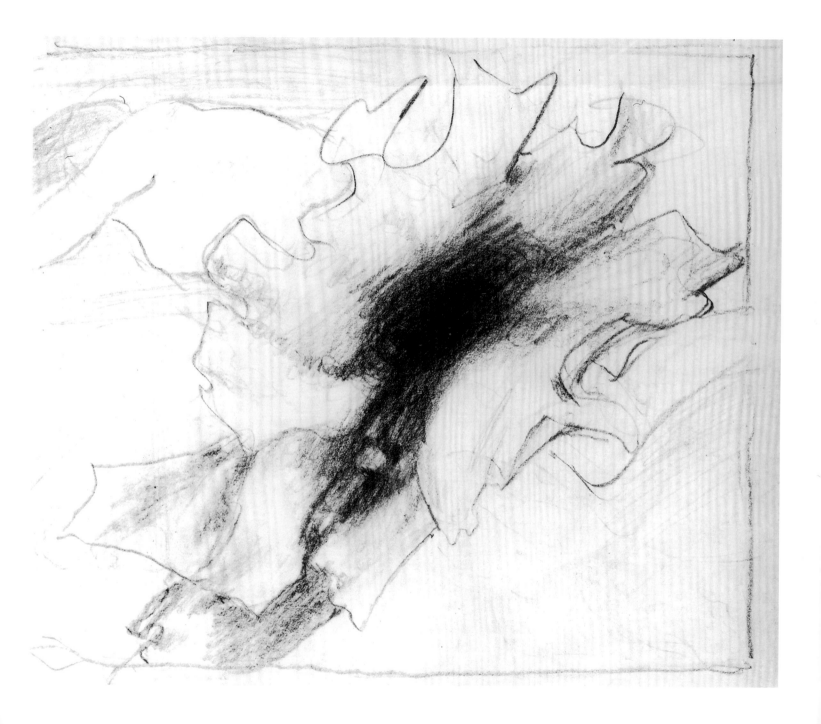

Cyanea barbellata

(Dalliance)

I offer hours of pain and pleasure mixed,
 black at heart, yet azure in the eye.
My thorns are few, and yet my thrall is fixed:
 no lover is my enemy.

Richard Howard

PLATE 7

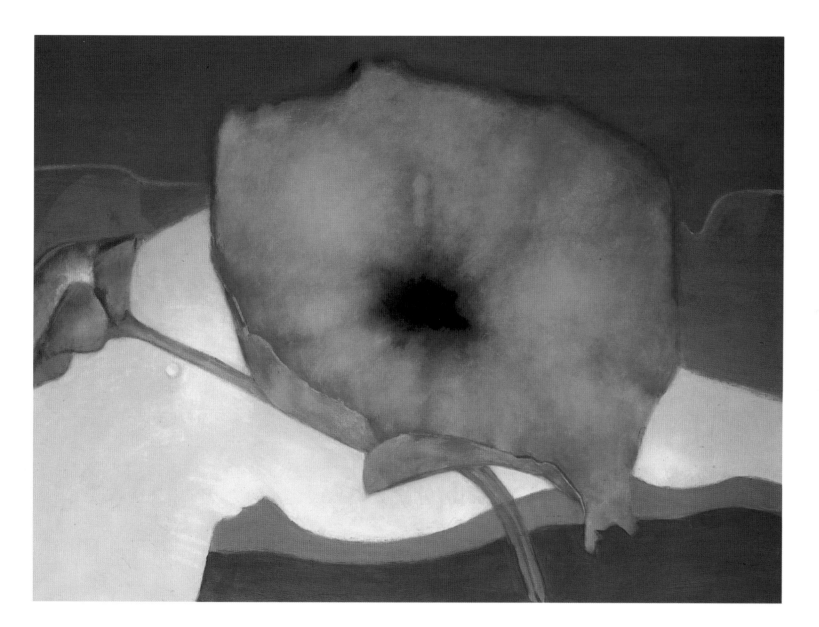

October 3

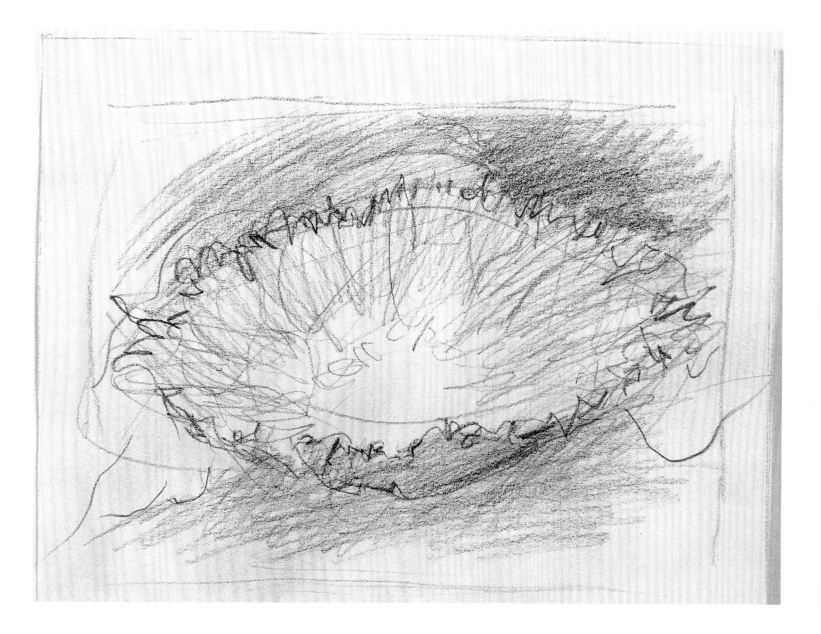

Nephaster cyaneus

(Cloudstar)

The sudden brightness at a nova's heart
Predicts a gradual, dimming ebb and flow
Of light — or love — that will in time depart,
Remembered only as desire's afterglow.
O dark mysterious flower, guard this night.
Keep her now from morning's cold insight.

J. D. McClatchy

PLATE 8

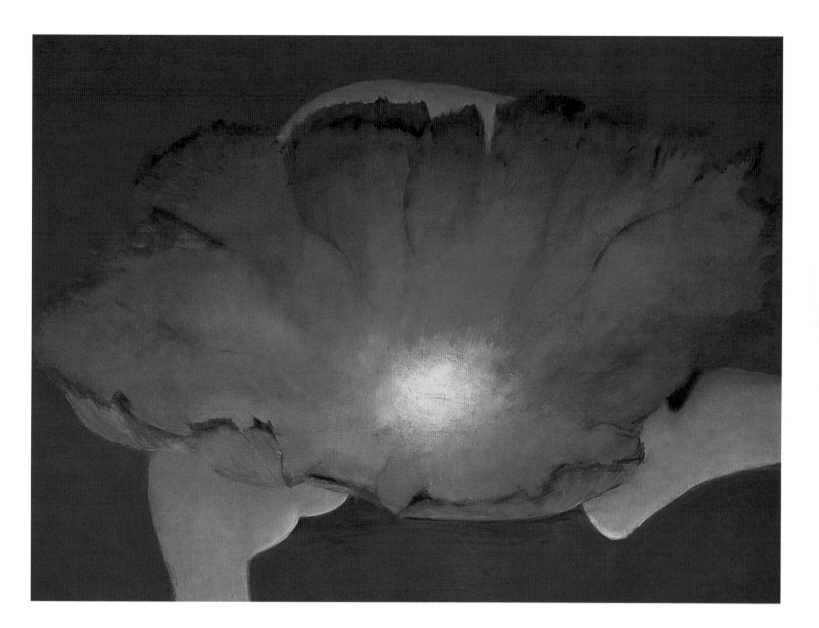

October 21

Crepuscula glacialis

(var., *Flos cuculi)*

I open before you
the time of the cuckoo
the vision of the dew
the white when the day is new
the brightness it passes through
the shadow it turns into
at the hour of the echo
from behind to mountain

W. S. Merwin

PLATE 9

November 18

Victrola floribunda

I am always shaking deliquescent bonbons
out of my hat. Is that a hat-trick?
I have never known what "hat-trick" means,
though I am sure there are many who do
and many more who do not.

John Ashbery

PLATE 10

December 29

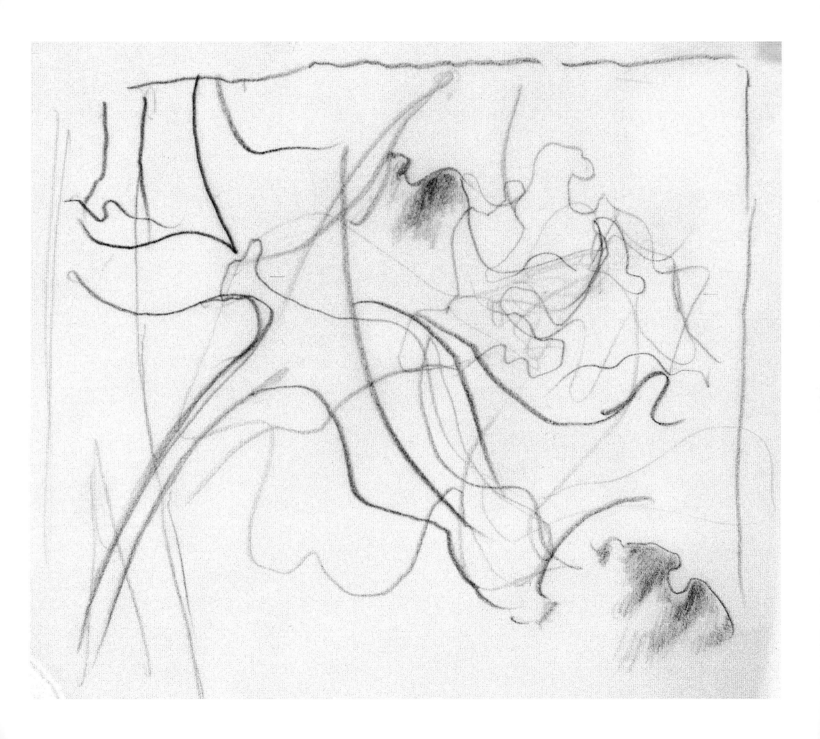

Flagrantis speculum veneris

(Loveknot)

I am flesh and flower
That each other devour.
Tongue-tied lovers know
It's myself I swallow.

Stephen Yenser

PLATE 11

February 5, 1998

Convolotus alchemilia

(Quiet-willow window)

smoke veil tissuing   in my thin
sugar, spread-veined & still
        so green-legged   for jumping through

Echo's silver glass to this
                        temple of birdrush
            crushed, edges smudged to blur

the violetly-loved body.   There

    you would   hear me.

Brenda Shaughnessy

PLATE 12

THE PAINTINGS

1. *Merrillium trovatum.* Oil on canvas. 56 x 66 in.

2. *Clog Herb.* Oil on canvas. 38 x 51 in.

3. *Starry Venusweed.* Oil on canvas. 38 x 51 in.

4. *Windwort.* Oil on canvas. 38 x 51 in.

5. *Burnt Umbrage.* Oil on canvas. 38 x 51 in.

6. *Griefbane.* Oil on canvas. 38 x 51 in.

7. *Dalliance.* Oil on canvas. 38 x 51 in.

8. *Cloudstar.* Oil on canvas. 38 x 51 in.

9. var., *Flos cuculi.* Oil on canvas. 38 x 51 in.

10. *Victrola floribunda.* Oil on canvas. 56 x 66 in.

11. *Loveknot.* Oil on canvas. 56 x 66 in.

12. *Quiet-willow window.* Oil on canvas. 56 x 66 in.

THE POETS ☿

JAMES MERRILL was born in New York City and lived in Stonington, Connecticut. The author of twelve books of poems, including *The Changing Light at Sandover* (Alfred A. Knopf, 1982), he also published two novels, two plays, a book of essays, and a memoir. His final collection of poetry, *A Scattering of Salts*, was published shortly after his death in 1995.

HARRY MATHEWS is the author of numerous works of poetry and prose fiction. His most recent novel, *The Journalist*, was published by David R. Godine in 1993. Raised in New York, Mr. Mathews spent the years from 1952 to 1978 in Europe. He currently divides his time among New York, Paris, and Key West.

ROSANNA WARREN studied painting at Yale University and received her MA from Johns Hopkins University Writing Seminars. She is editor of *Satura: 1962–1970* (W.W. Norton & Co., 1998), a collection of William Arrowsmith's translations of Eugenio Montale. Her third and most recent collections of poems, *Stained Glass,* was published in 1993. She teaches comparative literature at Boston University and lives in Needham, Massachusetts.

DEBORA GREGER, who grew up in Washington, is the author of five collections of poems, most recently *Desert Fathers, Uranium Daughters* (Penguin, 1996) and *Off-Season at the Edge of the World* (University of Illinois Press, 1994). She teaches at the University of Florida and lives in Florida and in Cambridge, England.

ADRIENNE RICH was born in Baltimore, Maryland. She is the author of more than fifteen volumes of poetry, most recently *Dark Fields of the Republic: Poems, 1991–1995* (W.W. Norton & Co., 1995). She has also published several volumes of prose, including *What Is Found There: Notebooks on Poetry & Politics* (W.W. Norton & Co., 1993). She lives in northern California.

ANTHONY HECHT's most recent book of poetry is *Flight among the Tombs* (Alfred A. Knopf, 1996). He is also the author of several volumes of literary criticism, including *On the Laws of Poetic Art: The Andrew Mellon Lectures in the Fine Arts, 1992* (Princeton University Press, 1995). He has taught widely, most recently at the Graduate School of Georgetown University. He lives in Washington, D.C.

RICHARD HOWARD was born in Cleveland, Ohio. He is the author of ten volumes of poetry, including *Like Most Revelations* (Pantheon, 1994). The translator of more than 200 works of French literature, he is also poetry editor of *The Paris Review* and of *Western Humanities Review*. He lives in New York City and teaches at Columbia University.

J. D. MCCLATCHY was born in Bryn Mawr, Pennsylvania. He is the author of four books of poetry: *Ten Commandments* (Alfred A. Knopf, 1998), *The Rest of the Way* (McKay, 1990), *Stars Principal* (Macmillan, 1986), and *Scenes from Another Life* (George Braziller, Inc., 1981). He has been editor of *The Yale Review* since 1991 and lives in Stonington, Connecticut.

W. S. MERWIN'S most recent collections of poems are *The Folding Cliffs* (Alfred A. Knopf, 1998) and *The Vixen* (Alfred A. Knopf, 1996). He is also the author of four books of prose and a distinguished translator of poems in several languages. Born in New York City, Mr. Merwin grew up in Union City, New Jersey, and Scranton, Pennsylvania. He is currently serving a five-year term as judge of the Yale Series of Younger Poets. He lives in Hawaii.

JOHN ASHBERY was born in Rochester, New York. He is the author of nineteen books of poetry, including *Wakefulness* (Farrar, Straus & Giroux, 1998). He has also written art criticism, plays, and a novel with James Schuyler. Mr. Ashbery is currently the Charles P. Stevenson, Jr., Professor of Languages at Bard College.

STEPHEN YENSER'S collection of poems *The Fire in All Things* was published by Louisiana State University Press in 1993. He is also the author of two critical books, *The Consuming Myth: The Work of James Merrill* and *Circle to Circle: The Poetry of Robert Lowell*. A native of Wichita, Kansas, he is a professor of English and director of creative writing in the English Department at UCLA.

BRENDA SHAUGHNESSY was born in Okinawa, Japan, and grew up in southern California. She recently completed her MFA in poetry at Columbia University. Her first book of poems is forthcoming from Farrar, Straus & Giroux in spring 1999. She lives in New York City.

RICHARD HOWARD was born in Cleveland, Ohio. He is the author of ten volumes of poetry, including *Like Most Revelations* (Pantheon, 1994). The translator of more than 200 works of French literature, he is also poetry editor of *The Paris Review* and of *Western Humanities Review*. He lives in New York City and teaches at Columbia University.

J. D. McCLATCHY was born in Bryn Mawr, Pennsylvania. He is the author of four books of poetry: *Ten Commandments* (Alfred A. Knopf, 1998), *The Rest of the Way* (McKay, 1990), *Stars Principal* (Macmillan, 1986), and *Scenes from Another Life* (George Braziller, Inc., 1981). He has been editor of *The Yale Review* since 1991 and lives in Stonington, Connecticut.

W. S. MERWIN's most recent collections of poems are *The Folding Cliffs* (Alfred A. Knopf, 1998) and *The Vixen* (Alfred A. Knopf, 1996). He is also the author of four books of prose and a distinguished translator of poems in several languages. Born in New York City, Mr. Merwin grew up in Union City, New Jersey, and Scranton, Pennsylvania. He is currently serving a five-year term as judge of the Yale Series of Younger Poets. He lives in Hawaii.

JOHN ASHBERY was born in Rochester, New York. He is the author of nineteen books of poetry, including *Wakefulness* (Farrar, Straus & Giroux, 1998). He has also written art criticism, plays, and a novel with James Schuyler. Mr. Ashbery is currently the Charles P. Stevenson, Jr., Professor of Languages at Bard College.

STEPHEN YENSER's collection of poems *The Fire in All Things* was published by Louisiana State University Press in 1993. He is also the author of two critical books, *The Consuming Myth: The Work of James Merrill* and *Circle to Circle: The Poetry of Robert Lowell.* A native of Wichita, Kansas, he is a professor of English and director of creative writing in the English Department at UCLA.

BRENDA SHAUGHNESSY was born in Okinawa, Japan, and grew up in southern California. She recently completed her MFA in poetry at Columbia University. Her first book of poems is forthcoming from Farrar, Straus & Giroux in spring 1999. She lives in New York City.